D1403070

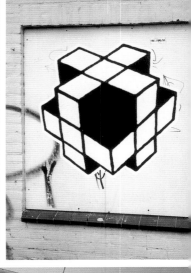

Thames & Hudson

STREET LOGOS

TRISTAN MANCO

CONTENTS

© 2004 and 2005 Tristan Manco

Individual logos copyright of the artists

All Rights Reserved. No part of this publication may be reproduced or transmitted in any form or by any means, electronic or mechanical, including photocopy, recording or any other information storage and retrieval system, without prior permission in writing from the publisher.

First published in paperback in the United States of America in 2004 by Thames & Hudson Inc., 500 Fifth Avenue, New York, New York 10110

thamesandhudsonusa.com

Reprinted, with revisions, 2005

Library of Congress Catalog Card Number 2003111315

ISBN-13: 978-0-500-28469-8
ISBN-10: 0-500-28469-5

Printed and bound in China by Hing Yip Printing

WATCH THIS SPACE

Graffiti art is constantly evolving. Each day, fresh coats of paint and newly pasted posters appear overnight in cities across the world. In a process of perpetual renewal, new marks and artworks are layered over the fading ghosts of graffiti past and the decaying surfaces of the city.

Ephemeral by nature, graffiti is an art form that celebrates change and feeds on new ideas. As artists unleash their creations, wall spaces become breeding grounds for new forms, techniques and tactics. New graphic and typographic strains emerge as ideas cross-pollinate. This book is a tribute to the new generation of innovators who, over the past few years, have been revolutionizing graffiti and our perceptions of it.

Today's graffiti landscape is fast becoming unrecognizable from that of previous decades with the emergence of an 'anything goes' approach. Artists have been creating more personal trademark signs and symbols, sometimes painted at monolithic sizes. Spontaneous doodles have run riot as sketchbooks are swapped for street corners. From the cryptic tags of São Paulo's *pixadores* ('taggers') to the stencil graffiti revolutions in Melbourne, the inventiveness and diversity is bewildering as artists and spectators are drawn to graffiti art as the ultimate free-for-all

communication. The aim of this book is to document today's graffiti gene pool, with its visual language of signs, icons, logos and characters.

Today's new style of graffiti challenges current definitions. Graffiti as personal mark-making can describe anything from a poster or painting to a plastic toy glued to a wall. In its narrowest interpretation, graffiti refers to the hip-hop graffiti writing that originated in New York in the late 1960s. Since graffiti is mainly associated with tags and pieces in this 'classic' style, other phrases have been coined for art produced on the street.

'Street art' is a term that was first used in the 1980s to describe any art in the urban environment not in the predominant hip-hop style. It rose to prominence in New York's SoHo through the work of painters like Keith Haring, Kenny Scharf and Richard Hambleton, and in Paris through artists like Blek and Némo. Seemingly a useful catch-all name, its 'fine art' or 'trendy' associations leave some artists feeling uneasy with the label.

Although some think that 'classic' graffiti has been stuck in a groove, a flick through some recent graffiti magazines or a visit to a local hall of fame makes it instantly obvious just how much has changed since the 1980s. In a revolt against generic styles,

artists are breaking the unwritten graffiti rules to create new graphic forms and images outside 3-D and wild-style lettering. Artists have been looking far and wide for new ideas, drawing inspiration from a huge variety of sources, including bio-technical forms, calligraphy, ethnic patterns, retro fashions and fine arts.

Artists are using new materials to reflect the surrounding urban environment, such as posters, stickers, acrylics, ceramics and collages, as well as computers to share art through the Internet. They have been colonizing and customizing new city spaces, like advertising billboards or abandoned vehicles, as well as inventing ingenious interventionist tactics to subvert cities' signage systems.

As former 'traditional' graffiti artists begin to use new techniques and paint in new ways it becomes more difficult to distinguish between 'street art' and 'graffiti'. 'Post-graffiti' and 'neo-graffiti' are more recent phrases used to describe street art and a graffiti scene in flux between established ideas and new directions. However, these abstract terms are rarely used and it is tempting to invent a new label. 'Brandalism' was first used by the artist Banksy to describe his 2003 exhibition in London, capturing the mood of antipathy towards corporate branding.

Art is not where you expect to find it Patrick Mimran

Opposite, clockwise from top Logos by Xupet Negre, Toasters, La Mano and D©, Barcelona

Hand by La Mano, Barcelona

Chalk drawing by Keith Haring, New York

It could also be used to describe graffiti artists who create their own personal signs and logos, resulting in a generation of 'brandals'.

Whatever the terminology, the urban environment attracts artists of all persuasions – train-writers, paste-up artists, performance artists, poetic doodlers, muralists and protest artists – whose collective work adds up to a city-wide graffiti message board of art and ideas.

Graffiti today is more visible, less cryptic and communicates to a wider audience. In cities choked with advertising it provides an important forum for social commentary and free expression. Its innovators enliven the urban landscape with bold graphics and extraordinary images, creating a new visual vocabulary – infused with contemporary graphic design and illustration but free from artistic constraints.

Fluent in branding and graphic iconography, graffiti artists have been replacing tags with more personal signs. Through artists like Barcelona's La Mano, with his trademark 'hand', the concept of tagging has evolved – the crypto-typography of tagged letters has been replaced with a stylized pictogram or logo.

Across the world these simple logo-tags or signs are becoming widespread, with each city having its own exponents. In New York you might find tags of alien-piloted UFOs, in Pisa envelopes, in Barcelona black sheep, coat hangers and closed-circuit televisions, to name a few. Some signs have self-evident meanings but others have more coded intentions. These signs join a lexicon of other ubiquitously graffitied emblems, such as the CND symbol or the love heart.

These logotypes or 'street logos' work on both ancient and modern principles, communicating to us without words, like the geoglyphic symbols carved into the landscape by the pre-Inca people of Peru or the icons on a mobile phone. The pictographic symbol has been at the heart of visual communication throughout history and in today's corporate culture it takes its ultimate form in the logo.

Logos can be powerful emblems representing many ideas and emotions. In today's climate of anti-globalization, the logos of corporate giants now carry with them negative, as well as positive, associations. We have a love–hate relationship with them; some we admire, others we vilify. The word 'logo' may have been tarnished, but the logos and symbols in street art are very much alive – looked upon as public brands or anti-logos flying in the face of the nefarious empires of corporations.

The use of signs, icons and logos in street art is not new. In the early 1980s Keith Haring created a whole 'urban mythology' of symbols, drawn with chalk on to the found surfaces of blacked-out billboards in New York subway stations. Dolphins, pyramids, UFOs and his trademark 'radiant baby' were just some of the iconic graphic signs that Haring

An image speaks a universal language, to any person of any age or ethnicity
Above

Lovers by OPT, Bordeaux

Street actions by Jerk, Jey, Veenom, L'Atlas and Obey, Paris

developed in his comic-strip-style compositions. These images were universally recognizable, so viewers could easily interpret their meaning and the stories they illustrated. Often displayed alongside posters promoting iconic visions of products, his cryptic icons provided an alternative way of looking at the world. Haring was not the first artist to use signs in his work, but he left us with the idea of using personal symbols or logos in art, which in turn influenced advertising, fashion and design. Twenty years later his iconographic approach, simple graphic lines and naïve creative spirit live on in the currently booming street art scene.

The original 'old school' graffiti artists didn't accept the way artists like Keith Haring and Jean-Michel Basquiat were labelled 'graffiti artists' as they clearly came from a different world. It was felt that the art establishment was buying into graffiti style, but refused to acknowledge those artists who created the graffiti culture. Over time, the contribution of these pioneering artists has been recognized and admired, but the uneasy relationship of the graffiti world with the art establishment and with those advertisers adopting the graffiti style still exists. These worlds are diametrically opposed but inexorably drawn together. Galleries, magazines and shops are controlled spaces. Graffiti art is uncontrolled, but the talent and energy coming from it is too compelling to be ignored. An exhibition or a compilation like this book has to find ways of presenting something that cannot be bought or sold – graffiti exists in one specific place with its own particular atmosphere for a limited amount of time and then disappears.

Although assembling this book has been an enlightening experience, there have been many potential hazards of misrepresentation. There are so many approaches to art in the streets that it is difficult to speak of a general visual language – graffiti is a creative force that refuses to be pinned down. New pieces are created every day and an encyclopaedic undertaking would be out of date before the ink was dry. Graffiti cannot be divided into simple categories, so the chapters that follow are only a guide to joining the dots between some of the most innovative work out there.

Graffiti is no longer routine; instead we expect the unexpected. A sense of discovery and the continual metamorphosis of the city space keep the viewer positive and open to new experiences. In watching the city walls, some common threads in today's street art and graffiti can be deciphered, but what unites the whole scene is the reclaiming of public space for public art. Graffiti art is free – made by people because they want to, not because they need to. Commercial values or tastes do not control the production of graffiti and so without these pressures it's one of today's most fertile art forms.

Watch this space!

Today's new graffiti movement is more focused on the world surrounding it and more alive than classical graffiti Olivier Stak

Cities all over the world are layered with signs, from shop fronts and billboards to traffic lights and road markings. As well as informational and commercial signs, most cities now have alternative signs of life: graffiti – unsanctioned art and messages that share the same space and speak to the same audience as official signs.

Graffiti often borrows from the aesthetics of signage and the jargon of advertising campaigns. The drop-shadowed letters of shop signs, the wild vernacular lettering styles of naïve hand-painted signs and neon lights are just some of the city signs that have influenced graffiti lettering, compositions and tactics.

Reclaiming the city space is often seen by graffiti artists as their main mission, either as a reaction against consumerist advertising or a need to make a personal mark on their environment. In the days of classic graffiti, artists painted trains and walls, but currently the search for new city spaces has propelled them towards signage.

On one level, signs have simply been another place to make marks, such as the recent sticker outbreaks on road signs. However, some of today's new graffiti artists have become attracted to the medium of signs themselves. The fascination for artists is what signs symbolize. They represent order, authority, consumer culture and the way our lives are regulated.

Artists have seen the potential to confuse, amuse and comment by subverting current signs or by boldly creating their own signs. With desktop publishing or a single pot of paint, the opportunity to create a whole set of new signs for the city is temptingly possible.

'Signs of Life' was the project of an American artist, Sonik, who did just that. Noticing that almost all the street signs in the Boston area had extra bolt holes drilled in them, he realized that with some plywood, acrylic paint and nuts and bolts, he could add his own signs to the poles. Since 1996, he has had fun installing over five hundred of them. Though he never removed or blocked any existing signs, his own were eventually removed.

In Paris, François Morel changed Métro signs to read *Protestez* ('protest'). In Stockholm, there was a city-wide campaign to change the sex of the familiar 'crossing man' to a woman, poking fun at sexism in signage. British interventionist artist Heath Bunting created decoy signs with prophetic messages like 'Evolution of Man Subverted by Fear'. These works all share an element of surprise through camouflage. They speak with the same authority as sanctioned signs, alerting us to the social control we take for granted.

Another kind of sign sabotage is known as 'subvertising' – the art of changing billboard signs, usually through spray-painted messages, to make a political statement. Pre-dating hip-hop graffiti, this type of cause-led action has become a mass movement, with magazines such as *Adbusters* devoted to its many forms. The same technique is being used by street artists making primarily image-based interventions on billboards.

For instance, Bristol artist Mudwig hijacks billboards with spontaneously painted embellishments. His Dr Seuss-style drawings add an element of surrealism to otherwise bland advertising campaigns.

Une Nuit, a collective based in Paris, went further by completely replacing billboards with custom-made posters by different artists. This project started in a squat as 'Implosion/Explosion', with three street artists painting on paper the exact size of publicity panels and exhibiting them in one place at rue Oberkampf.

In May 2002, they hatched a bigger plan. Sixty-three original panels from sixty-three different painters were prepared in the squat over three months. In the course of one night on 24 May, they covered the 11th arrondissement of Paris with posters.

The following year more than one hundred panels were displayed all over France. The artists came from a variety of backgrounds and included El Tono and Nuria, Olivier Stak, HNT, Jace, OPT, Tom Tom and L'Atlas.

By creating art in public places, artists draw attention to city spaces and re-examine areas thought to have had no artistic interest. They challenge the ownership of space by councils and corporations. They battle with the giant illuminated billboards, themselves just as much visual invaders of the city as graffiti. It is difficult to imagine the absence of advertising in our consumerist society, and when the Berlin Wall came down, billboards were one of the first signs of consumerism to spread eastwards.

Graffiti artists have been looking at the city in new ways, teasing its sign systems, even repainting road markings – nothing, within good reason, is off limits. By personalizing, customizing and subverting, artists are creating their own sign language.

Opposite Billboards by Tom Tom and L'Atlas, Paris

Above, clockwise from top left Protestez by François Morel, Paris; Doing What You're Told, Stockholm; Sign action by Peter Baranowski, Stockholm; Headless by Peter Baranowski, Stockholm; Evolution of Man Subverted by Fear by Heath Bunting, Bristol; Bus stop sign, Milan; Signs by Sonik, Boston

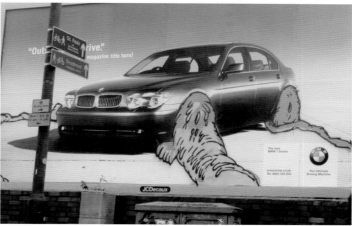

Above Paintings on found posters, by Mudwig, Bristol **Below** Diego by OPT, Bordeaux

13

This page Rastro by Cisma,
São Paulo

Opposite above Road markings by
Zevs, Paris

Opposite below Calligraphic signs
on road paint by Zys, Tokyo

ICONOGRAPHICS

In twenty-first-century graffiti there has been a shift from the typographic to the iconographic. It seems images speak louder than words. People have become immune to tagging, so when an artist starts using an image instead we suddenly take notice. Cut and pasted images of all descriptions have been appearing on walls around the world. Cardboard rocketships have landed in Melbourne, while in Stockholm robots made from Lego have invaded eaves of buildings. These images catch the eye among the visual noise of the street.

There is a limit to how much graffiti lettering alone can express, so in looking for other ways to communicate, artists have found that an iconographic approach speaks more directly to an audience.

Icons predate words, using the more emotive, visual language of symbols. Since the early pictograms of ancient peoples, symbols have been used to express all aspects of human life. Religious, cultural and scientific signs are all part of a vast universal library of iconic language. It's a graphic pick and mix to be plundered by both designers and artists. Pop icons can be juxtaposed with political icons. The head of Dopey the dwarf can be placed on the pictographic body of a revolutionary to create a new message, as seen in the work of Brooklyn-based poster artist, Bäst.

It is hard to say when or where icons were first used in graffiti as they are present throughout art. However, a mania for cut-out photocopies and stickers hit Holland with a vengeance at the end of the 1990s. Artists like Erosie, Influenza and Space 3 left tides of black and white images in their wake across the walls and street furniture of cities like Rotterdam and Eindhoven.

Their images of targets, flu flys and flying saucers were graphic explosions that experimented with both the repetition of images and a pictographic approach to graffiti bombing. These iconic cluster bombs were a new breed of graffiti, more graphic than tags, although dispersed in a similar way.

This new iconographic graffiti work bursts out of the city's architecture as the images are so unexpected against the urban surfaces; household appliances, animals, vegetables and desktop icons look as if they have escaped from a graphic zoo and gone to live wild in the city. The wilder or odder the images the better – the street is transformed into a strange storybook scene, a place more magical and less mundane.

These street icons are often cut out from photocopies or hand-painted paper to create the illusion that the image rests on the surface, an idea

Above Mural by El Cártel, El Tono and Nuria, Galeria Artificiel, Madrid

that we are accustomed to seeing on computer screens. The effect is heightened by leaving a white outline around the image or by adding a drop shadow. The solid black and white imagery cuts through the textural backgrounds of the city.

This iconic sabotage works on different levels for each artist. Pixel Phil, an artist from Bordeaux, makes visual jokes in the style of computer icons. The humour also comes from seeing his pixelated images outside in the environment, so his art makes a comment on the distance between the real and the computerized world.

Photocopied or screen-printed poster art itself is not new. Postered street art has been well documented through the 1980s in New York's SoHo and the student revolutionary posters of Paris in 1968. This activist spirit lives on in artists like El Cártel, a collective based in Madrid, who create posters using strong iconic images to explore social and political issues. Some traditions persist, but materials, techniques and approaches have changed,

signalling a new enthusiasm and era of experimentation with the medium.

Icons are not just used in single cut-out images or groups; they are part of a more graphic approach to graffiti, more relevant to today's society, using the familiar design language of advertising, desktop publishing, websites, video games and popular culture.

Iconic images are also used as brands or logos for artists. An iconic campaign becomes associated with an artist, such as Influenza's flu fly, and soon it becomes the artist's calling card. The logo as signature has become a growing trend in graffiti and at the root of this has been the graphic shift towards pictograms, symbols and icons.

The use of iconography is just one aspect of the work gathered in this section, and its artists would not define themselves solely through this idea. Through their common use of the language of symbols they have been creating some of the most intriguing, experimental and powerful art on the streets.

Following pages Top row: Deer by Peter Baranowski, Stockholm; Sheep Love, Barcelona; Horse, Melbourne; Duck and chicks by Flowerguy, New York; Paint pot poster by OPT, Bordeaux; Cake by TCF, Bristol; Paint bucket, Melbourne; TV men by Flowerguy, New York; 2nd row: Pacman by Pixel Phil, Bordeaux; Firestarter by Tom Civil, Melbourne; Head shot, Bristol; Robot by Gegganoja, Stockholm; Armchair by Marshall Artist, Sydney; Lotus flower by Betamaxxx, Eindhoven; Heart, Barcelona; Life is Art, Barcelona; Bottom row: Space Invader sticker, Paris; Fish stencils by Tom Civil, Melbourne; Escape hole by Pixel Phil, Bordeaux; Joystickers, Barcelona; Slot machine, Barcelona; Cut-paper rocket by Psalm, Melbourne; Radiation flower by Mambo, Paris; Spray-can by Eko, Pau

JOYSTICK

Joystick is a collective of Colombian artists based in Barcelona who promote experimental and multidisciplinary work. Their aim is to build new channels and spaces for communication. Recently, they have focused on public space intervention projects, mainly working with parasitic attacks of stickers and paste-ups.

One such project involved sticking printed paper images on trash containers. The idea was about rescuing and valuing items like used chairs and home appliances from the garbage. Joystick used simple illustrations of household objects with the message *Gracias a la basura que me ha dado tanto* ('Thanks to the trash that has given me so much') to comment on our wasteful society.

Another project was called Joystickers, presented at the Sound Art Festival of Barcelona, Zeppelin 2003. It invited people to mark with stickers places in Barcelona that they found interesting for the sounds that were produced or heard there. They had a choice of over 150 iconic vectorial images to make a graphical composition that depicted the sounds they encountered on the street. These sounds were then recorded and photographs taken of the corresponding walls.

ŤŤJOYSTICKERS

MAMBO

Born in Chile, Mambo now resides in Paris, where he has been painting both with and without the Alphabetick Force, of which he was a member from 1985 until its dissolution in 1997. Mambo has painted walls all over the world, including New York, Prague, Madras and Dakar.

Mambo's main influences are intellectual rather than visual. Political journalists and writers, such as Michael Moore, inspire him to express his opinions in humorous and original ways in both street art and design. Many of his ideas twist familiar icons to give them new meanings.

In prophetic paste-up actions made on burnt-out vans at the end of 2002, Mambo created cut-out symbols that parodied military and corporate ideas of power. In much of his work there are layers of interrelating symbols, logos and pictograms, which perhaps explains his fascination with the environment of desktop icons. In a series of melting portraits popping out from computer frames, he relocates the visual language of the computer on to the unsuspecting streets of Tokyo.

SPACE 3

Space 3 are two designer/illustrators who share a
studio in Eindhoven and have a long history of
producing street art. They needed a logo for a poster
and were inspired by a line from an Ultramagnetic
MCs song: 'We are the horsemen – enter your
spaceship!' This gave them the idea for 'Space'.
'3' came from the concept that when 2-D artwork is
hung in the streets it becomes 3-D. Hence Space 3.

Their original logo comprised three identical
spaceships above the words Space 3. It was later
reduced to the graphic icon of a UFO with jumbo
ears, a shape reminiscent of the spaceship-shaped
Evoluon building built in Eindhoven in 1966.

Space 3 play with the key elements of space
and the number 3 in their many graphic campaigns
to create a mysterious brand that exists only on the
street. They also work with other ideas, such as their
'tag posters'. These are designed to highlight the
much maligned art of tagging by providing posters
with box-shaped spaces for taggers to fill in the blanks.

VERBODEN TOEGANG

INFLUENZA

Influenza takes his name from a viral disease. The name well describes his interventionist actions in public spaces, such as retouching existing signs and adding useless information.

Originally from Paramaribo, Surinam, Influenza conducts his operations between headquarters in Paris and Rotterdam. Stickers are a perfect medium for his experiments. One of his many sticker projects was 'Illnesses and Diseases', a stark series of thought-provoking infectious words. He placed these black and white stickers in eye-catching clusters on the

streets – they seemed authoritative, as though plastered by an overzealous official.

In another action, Influenza used flu fly stickers to symbolize infection. They have since become the Influenza logo. The influenza virus, which almost wiped out the entire native American civilization, illustrates the link between the catastrophic spread of disease and the infectious spread of ideas. His work is an antidote to big budget manipulative advertising campaigns – Influenza is therefore a therapy, a medicine and a cure.

THE ART OF URBAN WARFARE

'The Art of Urban Warfare' was set up by Influenza as a collective game to promote street interventions in the name of art, under the motto 'the street belongs to us'.

Soldier shapes are sprayed with stencils on walls in three colours: green, blue or brown. Each participant chooses one of these colours and claims their turf. The game is open to participants in cities around the globe and battles are fought for territory as opposing armies meet. The formal structure of the game relies on collective participation and anonymity, so that opponents in the same town remain unidentified.

The winner of the game is the army with the strongest global coverage. The underlying aim is the conquest and free use of public space.

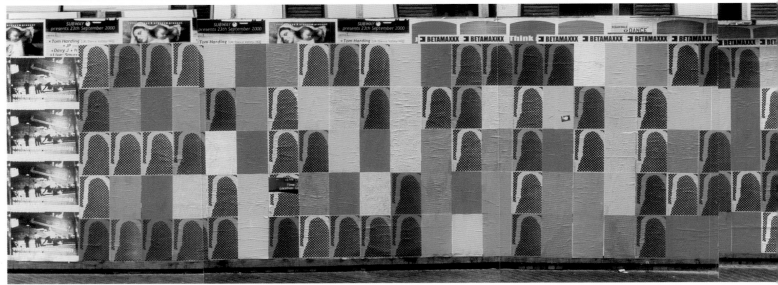

BETAMAXXX

Betamaxxx are Nanda, Rocs, PhetOne, Baschz and Crackrock, creative urban terrorists based in Eindhoven. They met through group projects within the Eindhoven underground music and art scene and gradually transformed into an explosive art collective, taking their name from a video format that failed in the consumer market.

Betamaxxx use a variety of media to comment playfully on contemporary mass culture. Their projects have embraced the Internet, urban interventions with stickers, posters and 3-D pieces, as well as increasingly ambitious installations with satirical video games, botanic gardens and mutant fairground attractions.

By mixing cultural icons, celebrities and consumer products with religious deities and symbols, Betamaxxx examine the way high- and low-brow culture coexist in the world. Their work draws attention to the way consumerism has become an alternative religion and to the mass production of global culture.

BÄST

For Bäst it all started in Flatbush, Brooklyn, in early 1983. Influenced by a Coney Island crew called BVD (Brooklyn Vandal Destroyers) and by early B-Boy style, Bäst started 'bombing' streets throughout New York. After starting a rudeboy posse called Helter Skelter in the early 1990s, Bäst dropped off the planet for about seven years. He then began to produce paper images from his bizarre ideas as a homage to his father who worked for thirty-five years in a paper factory.

His eclectic scrapbook of ideas, cut and pasted found images and odd words are combined in curious collages that perfectly suit the ephemeral nature of the posters themselves. Reminiscent of an electoral campaign, Bäst's name is emblazoned across the top of his posters, sometimes followed by the subtitle *Revolucion de Papel*. These campaigns have the aesthetics of rogue punk-style revolutionary posters.

FAILE

'Branding is a medium itself,' say Faile. 'We have all grown up in the advertising age. Big stars sell anything from mattresses to jock-itch creme; everything has a face on it. Everything has a campaign, an image, a lifestyle to sell – so many artists today communicate using the same methods of advertising and placement to command attention.

'We have taken branding, advertising and identity and have played with it. Our work is incredibly process driven, and samples bits and pieces from many different avenues. A lot of our work also tries to embrace duality – love and hate, violence and peace, the serene and the savage.

'Letting an image do the work and attaching our name or slogan of choice. This is where icons can say so much with so little, and there is a distinct beauty in that, a power. Letting the psyche fill in the gaps without the viewer being aware of it.'

FLOWERGUY

Michael De Feo, aka Flowerguy, has been creating artwork on the streets of downtown Manhattan since the early 1990s. He started off using the streets as a canvas for childlike imagery, such as moons, flowers and safety pins. Originally, these were made with stencils, but while brainstorming with a fat brush one day, a flower image stood out and he decided to turn it into a silk screen.

Screen-printing on to found paper, such as architectural blueprints and the pages of old atlases,

Flowerguy has produced thousands of flower prints over the past ten years. Hanging on various street surfaces, ranging from newspaper dispensers to buses, his flowers have become a familiar sight on the city streets. The iconic flower can be seen as a good luck charm for the city – a positive symbol that simply conveys the idea of creativity growing out of the urban environment.

PIXEL PHIL

Pixel Phil's work is rendered in the style of pixelated computer desktop icons. When displayed outdoors, his images clash with their setting; their virtual computerized aesthetic is juxtaposed with everyday reality.

Phil uses this iconographic style to make visual jokes, creating surprises and playing with our perception of images. Posters are his main medium, often cut out with fake shadows for added depth.

Phil particularly likes posters to have a connection with the place where they are pasted. He chooses the location before the poster and not the reverse.

EL CÁRTEL

El Cártel started in Madrid in 1999. The first poster was conceived to cover up some right-wing posters in the streets. That paved the way for other posters, always with the same format – four icons in a box, a mathematical equation of the theme, a title and then four drawings.

The posters are printed in editions of 500 copies in one colour, or two colours for special occasions. Everything is paid for by the artists and posted up in the streets so that there is complete freedom of speech. The drawings are by the group's four members: Olaf, Mutis, Eneko and Jaques le Biscuit. Their themes are mostly current affairs, things that really agitate them. This has included three wars, racism, real estate, physical abuse, immigration, advertising and elections, to name a few.

For the artists it doesn't matter who is drawing El Cártel. What matters are the content, the ideas and the freedom to express them.

EL CÁRTEL

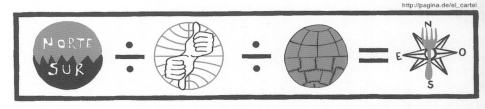

Nº MAL DISTRIBUÍDO

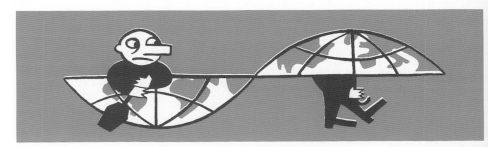

EL EMIGRANTE

N Ú M E R O P R I N G Á O

eneko.

MAREA NEGRA

UNO · MAS

MUTIS

2003

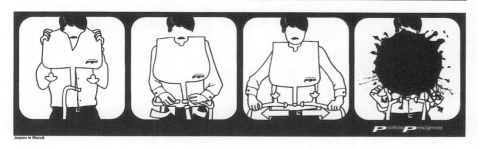

Jaques le Biscuit

Políticos Prestigiosos

---

http://pagina.de/el-cartel

N U M E R O C O M E M I E R D A

Presenting Jaques Le Biscuit's "The Birds" in Technicolour

¡ARRIBA LAS MANOS Y NO TE HAGAS EL GRACIOSO!

MUY BIEN. AHORA QUÉDATE QUIETECITO Y DIME DÓNDE LLEVAS TU MALDITO DINERO.

CAPITALISMO

PRODUCTO INTERIOR BRUTO

VISITE NUESTRO RESTAURANTE!

SUPER PLOMO €

EL GRAN NÚMERO MUNDIAL

CIRCO NEOLIBERAL

¡SALTA!

A LAS FIERAS DE HOY LAS DOMAN CON TELEVISIÓN.

PLUG

Plug is a Belgian artist who has been carrying out actions with his namesake, the European standard two-pin plug. The idea is to mix propaganda with a large dose of humour. He mainly adds painted plugs to machines or objects on the street so that they look unplugged, symbolizing the shutting down of the system.

Happy with the reaction caused by his painted plugs, he continued to experiment with this theme. His next scheme involved placing actual severed plugs in heroic situations, such as in the hands of a famous Belgian statue – the King Albert monument.

Plug's other exploits have included unplugging the traffic lights at a crossroad and putting a big pack of plugs in the middle of the street. He also created a dummy crime scene in which the outline of a dead body clutching a plug gives the impression that an electrician has been shot.

ETRON

Etron uses his own graphic symbol of a turd in the style of informational pictograms to make shitty visual jokes. He sees his work more as public puns and advertising hacking – less 'art' and more 'street fart'. The humour is base, but everybody gets the joke.

The shit symbol is pure slapstick and is used to indicate that something is crap – useful for slinging at the posters of politicians or unethical corporations. Etron uses this icon to get laughs, but also to vent his distaste at aspects of today's society and sometimes to highlight serious issues. For example, he has used the shit to comment on the turds of oil left all over the beaches by the capsized tanker Prestige.

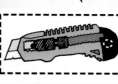

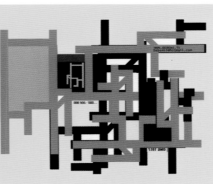

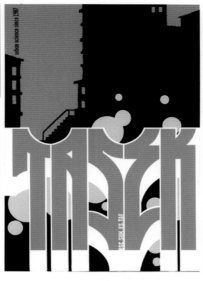
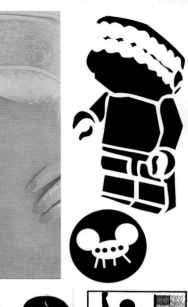

VIVA LA DESTRUCTION

urban science since 1997

MILK

YOUR ONE

WE ARE SHIT.COM

HOT!

REGULAR PRODUCT

1-INVADING
2-PUBLIC
3-PROPERTY

BFREE
ILLUSTRATE THIS MOTHERFUCKER

AUTHORISED RAFFITI AREA

BY ORDER NATIONAL HIGHWAYS AGENCY
APPLIES TO STICKERED SURFACE ONLY
EU DIRECTIVE 016/BNK/5Y

HAUT
JACE
BAS

COPY CREW

WWW.JONBURGERMAN.COM

LOGOS

Making your mark is the essence of graffiti culture. Writing your name or tag on walls, trains, or any available surface, is where it all began and continues to evolve. Graffiti taggers in the late 1960s began writing stylized names in their New York and Philadelphia neighbourhoods, sparking off an unstoppable craze. These tags were used to mark out territories, either by gangs or by individuals looking for recognition from other budding graffiti artists or from the world at large.

A tag is a small advertisement for an artist – a logo for the ego. To achieve greater street fame, artists added eye-catching devices to the ever-evolving letter forms, such as stars, crowns and quotation marks. In order to stand out from the crowd, tags became more elaborate, eventually evolving into bubble lettering and finally into the larger graffiti productions, known as 'pieces'.

Over time, tags became more about personal style and less about legibility. Graffiti writers had developed a highly sophisticated level of urban calligraphy whose audience largely came from within its own ranks. By the end of the 1980s some graffiti artists felt that tags and styles of writing had become too standardized and started looking for new inspiration. Faces, characters and abstract shapes began to leap out from the seas of spray-paint as artists changed their signatures to more iconic logos.

As represented in the previous chapter, graffiti has been converting to more graphic approaches as artists try to express new ideas to a wider audience by using icons and other visual devices. An icon depicts an idea but it can also be used as a logo. The only difference is the artist's intention. A logo is a unique symbol or design that represents a company or person. If an artist creates and repeats an image as a signature mark often enough – it could be the number 6, a giant doughnut or a hand – it becomes a tag or logo.

At the start of the 1990s there were just a few noticeable logos, but today a jungle of pictograms, abstract shapes and mysterious characters has spread across our streets, creating a new graffiti ecosystem. These new signs are spray-painted, drawn, stencilled, postered and stickered, with visual aesthetics unique to each artist. From comic books to fine art, each artist brings his or her own influences to the mix. Unlike tags these new 'logo-tags' and iconic images do not follow style elements that have gone before. Instead they adopt a 'what hasn't been done before?' attitude, going beyond what we recognize as graffiti.

Artists' signs and logos don't have to perform a commercial function and so can break the rules of branding by changing and adapting their signs with each rendition. Altering your logo each time can be a virtue. El Tono and Nuria are artists from Madrid whose signs change in each work. Their signs – respectively a 'tuning fork' and a 'key' – are made up of hand-painted cubist lines that twist and turn in relation to the underlying surfaces but still resemble the original shape. The idea is that the work is slightly hidden and encrypted and the observer's enjoyment can come from unravelling the code.

For some artists, creating a brand presents an opportunity for rogue campaigns that parody advertisements. Based in Los Angeles, the renowned artist Shepard Fairey used the unlikely image of a wrestler called André the Giant to create an alternative brand through street actions. Like Big

Brother in George Orwell's *1984*, the giant stares out at the public, accompanied by the word 'Obey'. The message can be seen as anti-social control or anti-advertising. Ironically, due to a huge cult following, the Obey campaign unwittingly became a global brand itself, which, in terms of controlling the public arena, was a triumph.

The artists represented in this chapter tend not to be overtly political, although the politics of freedom operate as their images are freely viewed in competition with advertising and in some cases they hijack billboard spaces. They have appropriated certain aspects of branding, such as local and global campaigns and the use of repetitious logos, to get their ideas across but they are more like artists' own-labels than graffiti super-brands – more human and genuine than commercial logos. They are not trapped by their own brand that they must repeat ad infinitum. These artists are free to begin new campaigns when inspiration strikes and as viewers we eagerly await their new pieces.

Present day advertising has used repetition to create some of the most powerful and globally recognizable symbols, such as the colours of Coca-Cola and the swoosh of Nike. In Cuba, where very little graffiti exists, the Nike swoosh is drawn by kids as an envied symbol of Western consumerism, whereas in the capitalist world the current atmosphere of corporate disenfranchisement leads to commercial logos being graffitied over or blanked out. As commercial logos lose their shine and cities start to look the same, graffiti street signs and logos become a symbol of individuality, fulfilling man's basic urge to leave a trace on the world.

Opposite, from left to right Logos by Sam Bern, HNT, Miss Van, Poch and Olivier Stak, Paris

ABOVE

In 2000, Above started to paint his name on freight trains. One day, he saw one of his pieces passing by too fast to read and realized that to have any impact his artwork had to grab the viewer's attention instantly.

'We live in a world heavily saturated by logos,' says Above. 'For instant recognition, advertisers use images as opposed to a name. Images speak a universal language to captivate viewers of any race or age. So I shifted from conventional letters to an icon that would fit the name Above – the most familiar image known to man, an arrow. I am now referred to as the guy that paints arrows. More than

the name, people can relate to the arrows, which are open to individual interpretation.'

Above has used stickered, stencilled and spray-painted arrows to 'pierce' the cityscapes of Paris and San Francisco. More recently he has attached small wooden arrows to buildings and hung arrow mobiles just above head height.

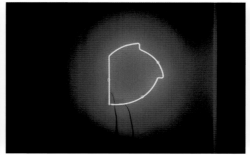

OLIVIER STAK

Stak started painting at the end of the 1980s, but he was always attracted to ideas outside traditional graffiti art. In 1995, he transformed his tag into a logotype image so that it would stand out from all the others. He began to see it as 'wild advertising' and experimented with the placement of his logo in relation to the city space. In a radical move away from decoration to pure form, this logo has been reduced to a single colour with a simple silhouette shape.

Stak continued to work in different ways. While exhibiting in Paris in 1999, he first used neon to present his logo, combining the idea of street signage with his rogue graffiti symbol. He is also interested in the relationship of street art with the art, fashion and media worlds. The fashion industry has always taken inspiration from the street, but often graffiti is used only as decoration. With his 'Most Hated/Loved' ironic painted statements, Stak wanted to reflect how graffiti is loved by media darlings when its services are needed but still remains criminalized.

TOASTERS

The Toasters are three single-minded and like-minded individuals based in the UK. Since 1999, they have been promoting the image of a pop-up toaster on street corners around the world. It's an enigmatic image that can be viewed differently on each encounter and is open to interpretation: it could be a secret sign, a surrealist brand or a logo for a non-existent product.

Through steadfast campaigning, more people outside the graffiti world have been discovering the toaster and are curious and bewildered by its reoccurrence. However, the Toasters continue to experiment with their creation.

AVIADRO

Aviadro began making street art in 2000, after meeting graffiti artists at college in Barcelona, where he was studying graphic design. He shared their enthusiasm but didn't want to make conventional graffiti. He confesses that this was partly because of his own potential incompetence, but also because he wanted to produce something personal.

With his friend Oldie, he formed the Artistas Superfluos Crew, whose work was always jokey and surreal. They followed no preconceptions and used whatever technique came to mind, such as latex paint, plaster and silver foil. Later, Aviadro met the ONG collective and immediately identified with their attitude — they put experimentation and thought into their works, murals with an idealistic party atmosphere.

Aviadro's work is based around images of 'living machines', repeated like a tag, on a large scale with paint and a roller, or as part of murals. They represent his love–hate relationship with progress and his rejection of the humanization of machines.

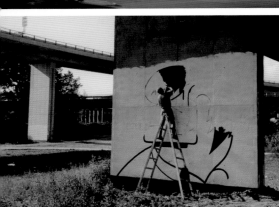

HNT

'Urbanism/brutalism. Proud façades, arrogant faces. A long black line in the curve of which a Metro sleeps. Stars in the eyes, in the palm of the hand, and on the fingertips, metallic dust. Red like a wound, a scar which will be repainted at dusk. And in the mind, a little song by Nico: *I'll Be Your Mirror.*'

XUPET

Xupet Negre means 'black dummy' and this simple icon has been a part of graffiti life in Barcelona since 1989. It is hard to imagine Barcelona's vibrant and progressive painting scene without the signs, symbols and logos that now proliferate, but at one time Xupet was alone in his approach of repeating a single mysterious and anonymous sign.

To some extent, signs were already an element of local street art in the city. Visiting artists like Keith Haring were also an influence, but it was Xupet's campaign that signalled change in the scene.

Over time, Xupet's dummy has been taken up as a city mascot, and he has begun to add figures and positive messages to his pieces, such as: Peace, Love, Respect, Equality and Freedom.

SUMS

Sums is the alter ego of a Bristol-based pro-skateboarder who began painting graffiti with his older brothers at about eight years of age. In the past two years he has been painting and stickering his symbol – the paw. The paw is intended to be a soft, fun image, a symbol that reflects his personality.

The paw started small, as stickers and stencils the size of a cat's paw print. Over time, the sign got bigger and began to mutate as he played with the components of the shape. The campaign remains anonymous, bold and intriguing. There are no messages – just follow those paw prints and observe the city.

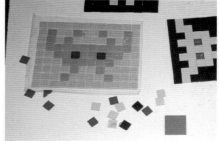

SPACE INVADER

For some time mosaics representing the aliens from the old video game Space Invaders have been appearing in big cities. This movement is led by an anonymous Parisian, aka Invader, who wants his mosaics to invade the world. London, Paris, Tokyo, New York and Melbourne have all been attacked. Maps are produced of these conquered cities as souvenirs that help people locate the mosaics – sometimes there are as many as one thousand unique sites in a single city.

The mosaic is a perfect addition to the cityscape, working well with its structures and materials. Invader picks his sites carefully, finding hidden spots where the artwork is camouflaged. More permanent than other street actions, the Space Invader mosaics could have a place in architectural history for centuries to come. Or is this just the beginning of a bigger invasion plan?

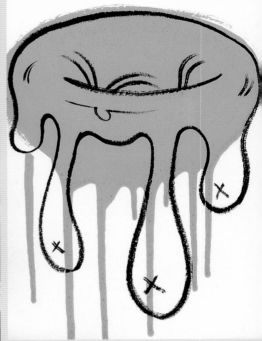

MAYA HAYUK

Maya Hayuk was raised by Ukrainian immigrant parents in a suburb of Baltimore, converting to punk rock at an early age. After extensive travel throughout the US and Europe, Maya earned a BFA in Conceptual Art and Philosophy.

She started off photographing musicians, playing in bands, designing posters and painting murals in nightclubs and on the streets. Maya has also curated shows and worked in collaboration with Banksy, the Barnstormers, Graphic Havoc and 9th Concept from Paris.

Relentlessly populist in her approach to making and disseminating art, Maya hand-paints stickers and comics, which she distributes anonymously. One of her most appealing images is her trademark pink doughnut, which she either hand-paints on to walls, prints or draws on to stickers. Like freshly dripping paint, these home-made doughnuts make a splash on the street with their appetizingly simple yet bold appearance.

SANTY

On the corners of buildings all over Milan can be found the suprising image of a balcony. Painted quite freely with two or three colours, this is the signature work of Santy.

It's a drawing that fits the atmosphere of this Italian city but an unusual one among graffiti artists. Santy explains, 'the balcony is a detached point of view, far from the bustle of the square. Someone is living inside the balcony; the story of this "person" is ancestral and charming – a heartbeat of humanity.' The viewer, in fact, can bring his or her own story to it – the image is 'open'.

His work is also concerned with the actions of hands and feet – with the notion that the movements and the posture of a body are a map of a person's personality. He chooses these human stories as a way of looking at our daily lives and as a reminder that we live by the power of our actions.

LA MANO/NAMI

La Mano is an artist with a cult following. Visitors to the Barcelona area will be familiar with his work, but his trademark hands can also be found in cities such as Madrid and Milan. Also known as Nami, his hand has become his personal identity sign.

La Mano paints with a passion that you can feel in his work. The hands appear in so many forms and places, from a simple line drawing in a dark corner to a gigantic hand on a wall or on top of a building. La Mano sometimes interweaves characters into his designs, such as figures in space helmets or television screens and often repeats and loops his hands to form complicated mazes. He also collaborates with other Barcelona graffiti artists, like Sixe, under the collective name Art Attack.

The hand is a symbol that everyone can understand and La Mano loves the way people who are not graffiti writers can recognize his mark.

108

108's amoeba-like creation originated in Alessandria, Italy, but has travelled to cities such as London, Paris and New York.

108's first graffiti experience was with tags, but he soon decided to experiment with other ideas. The minimal amoebic form is inspired by pure shape. Its highly visible acid-yellow colour bites into the cityscape. Like a playful alien snail trail, its shape is mutable but always recognizable.

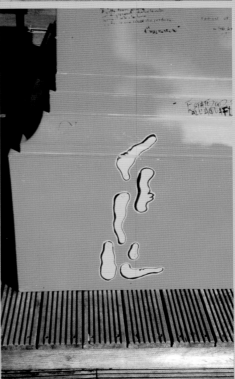

SICKBOY

At the beginning of 2000, strange domed temples began to spring up like mushrooms on the street corners and trash containers of Bristol. They were the start of a graffiti phenomenon known as Sickboy.

Sickboy is interested in what the artist Hundertwasser called the natural restoration of the city. The organic shapes and freehand lines of his painted temples imitate nature in the way they flow against and contrast with the structured lines of the city.

Sickboy sees his work as friendly graffiti that speaks to a wide audience. Although no two temples are exactly the same, the concept is an easily identifiable logo. The consistent use of a red and yellow colour scheme reflects the deliberate colour theory behind many corporate logos. Not only do these bright colours stand out against the gritty urban backdrop, but, like the McDonald's brand, they make the temples instantly recognizable.

KAMI

Kami grew up at the foot of a mountain in Kyoto. His house stood close to a temple, bordered by trees and a bamboo grove. It is these surroundings, as well as his experiences, that have influenced his art. He now lives in Tokyo, where he paints both on canvas and in the landscape.

Kami works with very loose overlaid lines and shapes, painted in harmony with their location. The shapes reflect his thoughts and the lines are inspired by the simplicity of traditional Japanese art. He prefers to display his art in public spaces, but sometimes paints private works, if he feels he can make a place prettier.

Kami is also known for his work as a member of the Barnstormers, a painters collective. Founded by New York painter Skwerm, the collective was originally formed to decorate barns in North Carolina with the help of local artists. Both with and without the Barnstormers group, Kami now makes painting tours all over the world.

SAM BERN

Sam Bern's work covers an unusual range of locations, beginning in Paris but later expanding to embrace the cities of Boston, Philadelphia and Beirut. He has created a new form of writing, which was born in the street and coats the city with lingering images like footprints or tattoos.

Bern's designs appear all over the city – on walls, pavements, boarded-up shops, billboards and subway stations – and in a variety of media, including acrylic, poster paint, screen-printing, stickers and stencils. These 'signs' cannot be decrypted or reduced through analysis with standard tools; they are like a basic form of language inspired by urban codes and signals.

EL TONO & NURIA

El Tono (the tuning fork) and Nuria (the key) make discreet urban space invasions based on the graphic codes of their respective symbols.

These shapes are the starting points for trails of brightly coloured blocks, which complement the faded paint and worn surfaces they are painted on. They always try to integrate their compositions with the architectural background and all the surrounding features.

It all began in around 1997 when El Tono moved from Paris to Madrid. He found the place so graffiti-saturated that he wanted to create something that would communicate with people in a simpler way. His answer was the tuning fork. At first these were roughly sprayed tags but gradually they became sharper and more refined. Later he met his girlfriend Nuria and now they nearly always work together. They enjoy the participation of pedestrians, who at first may not notice their signs, but once they have discovered them they are 'hooked' and want to find more.

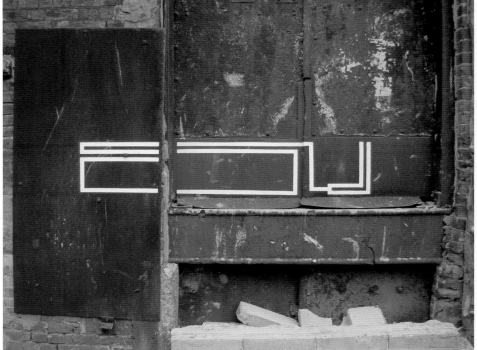

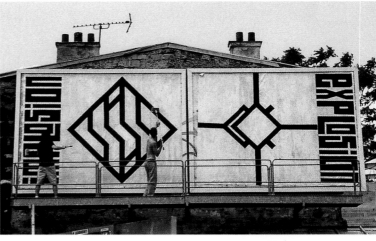

L'ATLAS

L'Atlas first got into tagging at about twelve years of age and later at high school in Paris he began to use the name Atlas. After leaving school, he travelled to Brazil, where he realized that 'atlas' was an international word. This made him want to make his work as universal as possible. To keep himself unique, however, he added the definite article to his name and became L'Atlas.

From the start L'Atlas's main interest was lettering. On returning from South America he went to college to study archaeology. Prompted by his growing interest in the history of writing he began to learn Arabic calligraphy. He wanted to combine traditional concepts with contemporary techniques in his work, and his use of only black and white is a reflection of this link with the past. His straight lines and geometric style reflect the traditional Kufic script, which is highly geometricized.

His trademark signs are various renderings of a compass, embodying the theme of universality. From billboard spaces to stamps and stickers, L'Atlas has been getting his work out to all corners of the globe. In 2001, he put his spray-paints away and began to mark out compass designs in the streets with gaffer tape. By chance, the summer heat made the tape bond with the Paris pavements so the designs are almost indelible.

URBAN CHARACTERS

Heroes, villains, monsters, figures and portraits of all descriptions populate our street corners. They live with us on our walls. Like passers-by, they are part of our daily experience. We share with them the alternative visual universe invented by their creators.

Characters have always played a part in the production of traditional graffiti. Initially they were taken from comic books. The most imitated work was by American cartoonist Vaughn Bode, whose art was made popular by writers like Dondi and Seen. His laid-back characters and fantasy worlds are classic graffiti iconography that almost define the genre. The fluid style of his line work also influenced the development of graffiti lettering.

Today artists no longer feel restricted by the limitations of Bode-inspired, generic styles. Instead they are taking more individual approaches to figurative graffiti art.

Artists like San Francisco's Barry McGee took inspiration for his characters from everyday street life. In the mid 1980s, as 'Twist', he began painting

large-scale images of ambivalent-looking urban characters observed from the forgotten and dejected denizens of the city. His characters were not just decorating murals but told their own story. This approach to figures is now widespread. Whether influenced by Twist or not, figures are painted without texts or backgrounds, simply existing on the texture of the walls.

Techniques and styles vary wildly from the simplest doodle to finely detailed masterpieces, freely painted or on posters, stencils and stickers. Figurative images can be one-offs. Others are part of a distinct series or world of characters, and some artists concentrate on repeating one image like a logo.

The character as logotype follows the trend towards logos in street art and mirrors the ubiquitous use of characters elsewhere in art and design, including comics, skateboard art, T-shirts and computer games. In commercial terms, characters can become global icons. The cute image of a cat like Japan's Hello Kitty can sell anything. Urban characters – unlike their wealthy, slickly packaged commercial cousins – are hobos, roaming the streets rather than adorning the front of a kid's exercise book.

Figures or characters, be they animal or vegetable, are the vehicles for ideas, with an endless scope for possibilities depending on the artist's intention. They can engage us on all kinds of levels: emotionally, humorously and politically.

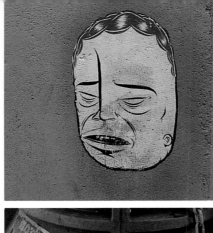

HEADS

Opposite, clockwise from top left Couple by Rep1, New York; Painted face by Twist, London; Stencilled face, Melbourne; Stencilled stickers, Adelaide; Love and Hate by Cre, Toulouse; Head, Canada; Skull poster, London; Heads by Pavia, Robot Inc. and Ozmo, Milan; Woman's head, New York; Stencilled face, Melbourne; Face, Canada; Sprayed face, Barcelona

Above Top row: Sprayed heads, Melbourne; Head by Skwerm, New York; Head detail by Sixe Crew, Barcelona; Repeated heads by Sixe Crew, Barcelona; 2nd row: Foaming head by Flan, ONG and NMD Crew, Barcelona; Head by J. Loca, Barcelona; Head by Feek, Bristol; Bottom row: Girl by Aiko, London; Repeated heads by Sixe Crew, Barcelona; Head detail, Barcelona

FIGURES

Opposite Top row: Masked boy, Barcelona; Stencilled boys, Barcelona; Figure with circles by Tom Civil, Melbourne; Postered face by Girig, Stockholm; 2nd row: Disguise by Sonik, Chalon; Figure with toaster by Mr Kern, Barcelona; Green dude by Mr Yu3, London; Bottom row: Crouched figure, Stockholm; Figure with Molotov cocktail by Os Gemeos, Sydney; Figure by Tom Civil, Melbourne

Above Top row: Chimp-headed woman by Faile, New York; Sweatshop by Eko, Pau; Don't Be Scared by Dlux, Melbourne; Kid character by Gorkingcrazy, Barcelona; Bottom row: Action Hero, Mumbai; Reclining figure by Human Lost, Tokyo; Character by Miss Van, Barcelona

AKROE

Paris-based artist and designer Akroe finds neglected spaces the perfect place to display his ideas. His first experiments with graffiti were at the age of five. Inspired by the television series Zorro, he began to use its name as a tag. However, his father's negative reaction brought his graffiti development to an abrupt halt.

Using the name Akroe, he returned to graffiti through the more illustrative approach of his geometric character designs. These mainly take the form of heads, crisply painted as cut-outs on to the wall space, using the natural textures as a background.

Although each character is different, they come from a recognizable mould – a mixture of bold lines and finely executed expressions, reminiscent of the angular graphic styles of 1950s and 1960s cartoons. Painted in forgotten spaces, they appear like cartoon mascots, guardians for faded and abandoned real estate. Akroe often paints with fellow artist KRSN to create clusters of interacting creatures and characters.

KRSN

In around 1998, KRSN began to make a switch from classic graffiti to something more personal, merging his love of graffiti with his love of illustration. By that time in Paris, where he is still based, artists like André, Zevs, HNT & Stak had already shown that new approaches were possible. KRSN began refreshing his own ideas.

It started with some stickered images he put on the street. He soon realized that people who knew nothing about graffiti had started noticing them. He gradually moved on to more elaborate, larger scale painting. Rather than a fixed logo identity, KRSN was attracted to the idea of a visual code – his own illustrative language that was recognizable but flexible. Through continuous drawing he has built up a world of quirky balloon-like animals, creatures and masked figures.

ALEXONE

Alexone is a graphic artist, working freelance as part of the 9th Concept collective in Paris. He is also known as Oedipe – the tag he uses for his abstract graffiti calligraphy.

Alexone's output is prodigious. He has undertaken countless solo missions and many collaborative works with his characters and stylized letters, working with artists like Jace, Gomes and the GM Crew. He has a reputation as one of the funniest and most amenable guys on the block and this comes across in his characters.

He describes his work as simple and funky, executed in clear lines and flat colours with a seriously oddball cast of characters. Elephants, penguins and other animals are some of his favourites. In Paris, a city with a low tolerance of graffiti artists, he has pioneered a technique of hand-painted cut-out posters, which can be applied quickly but tragically, like freshly baked croissants, they have only a short shelf-life.

ANDRÉ

André started producing graffiti around 1985, originally writing just his name. Although for him the act of painting the walls illegally is more important than the result, in 1989 André invented Monsieur A. This eccentric, long-legged character made his debut in the streets of Paris. Monsieur A runs, jumps and flies across the city — its walls and surfaces are the background to his own imaginary narrative.

For him the idea was the same as writing his name, but it was a drawing that everyone, young and old, could understand and enjoy. In those days, this was a completely new approach to graffiti. Although tags had sometimes included a simple figurative element, André was the first in the graffiti world to transform a character into a personal logo.

At first, other graffiti artists found Monsieur A strange, but slowly they were inspired by the concept.

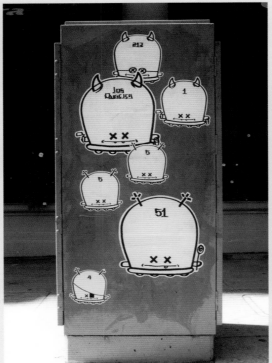

BUFF MONSTER

Buff Monster's eye-patched aliens were born from a night's inspired drawing session and the memory of a sticker from the 1984 Tokyo Expo, which had remained lodged in his brain since he was six years old.

Buff Monster makes cameo appearances in the soap opera that is the Los Angeles graffiti scene. He works mainly with posters and stickers, as well as with painted flattened spray-cans: 'Writers here appreciate the work I've put in, but I don't expect anyone to admit that they like the Buff Monster. It's probably too cute and pink for most hardcore writers. But girls like it.'

'The one aspect of street art that I really appreciate is the issue of ownership. Those who have it (property owners) don't want it, and those who want it (other artists) can't have it. My most recent paintings are the closest to my vision. They really drive home the indulgent, over the top, ridiculous candy land inspired by rock 'n' roll, ice cream, porn and LA. I really think that LA needs more pink clouds and if I don't do it, then no one else will.'

CHA

Cha – the cat – is based in Barcelona and studied painting at the Académie des Beaux-Arts in Paris. Cha has made a splash on the graffiti scene with a style that is partly inspired by his studies in the fine arts. His funky naïve cats are influenced by Chagall, Miró, Picasso and primitive art, as well as by the energy of early 1980s wild-style graffiti.

Cha's unaffected approach celebrates the act of painting on the free canvas of the city. The cat takes on many shapes and sizes, ranging from the smallest sticker to gigantic mural-sized cats filled with many smaller cats.

PEZ

Pez began painting in early 1999 and in a small space of time became both well known and highly prolific in his home city of Barcelona. At first he wrote the word *pez* ('fish') in letters and drew a fish next to it. After a while he became less interested in the letters and more influenced by the logos that were appearing in Barcelona, such as those of Craneo, La Mano and Xupet Negre. He then concentrated on the idea of the fish as a logo. Pez joins a menagerie of logos of animal forms in Barcelona, such as Cha and Birdy, who are among his many collaborators.

EL TIÑAS

El Tiñas translates as 'the stain' and is the alter ego of an up-and-coming artist from Vigo in Spain. For him the street has always been an inspiration, from its structural possibilities to wandering stray dogs on heat, and he enjoys working in these shared spaces as he is able to reach a wide variety of people.

The main motifs in his work are the black circles, which he features inside his carefully crafted characters or applies directly to the 'evil surfaces' (buildings). These circles represent empty minds and suffering brought on by human progress or disease. These sad visions have a more hopeful message behind them, which is to make people think like human beings and not like machines, and to remind them that they have a soul.

PELUCAS

Pelucas is the twin brother of Tiñas and the mastermind behind many curious characters pasted on the walls of his current hometown of Vigo. He has been drawing since he can remember, influenced by comic books like *Mortadelo and Filemon*. Drawing is his sanctuary and he spends ages doing many versions of the same drawing, looking for the definitive one.

His characters have a look of naïve innocence, but they are part of a sinister world of crazed evil, frequented by giant mobile phones using humans to speak, walking brains and the Grim Reaper. Through his characters' peculiarities and different facial expressions he wants to transmit both positive and negative emotions to the people passing by.

He sees his work as 'free publicity', more personal than the advertisements that bombard people every day. He feels that graffiti is the purest form of artistic expression, following the authentic and instinctive evolution of art. It goes to the very beginning of everything and is spontaneous and free.

NANO4814

Nano4814 is from Vigo in Spain, where he is currently studying 3-D design. As a prolific sketchbook doodler he was always creating new characters, which eventually found their way on to the streets. In around 1995, he started bombing walls with images of pigs and cows and became known as the guy who did the pigs. Rather than stick with the pigs, he began to look for an icon that represented himself and was drawn to 'El Choquito'

(The Squid). The squid squirting its black ink across the city suggested writing and creation and this became his personal signature.

Over time, Nano has begun to create new characters, such as the Puppeteers – bearded revolutionaries holding their fists up high in a gesture of power. However, he always tries to incorporate El Choquito in the action as well.

ADAM NEATE

Since 1999, Adam Neate has been producing 'Free Art' around the streets of London. He either leaves a single or a whole series of paintings leaning against walls or hung on random nails.

Neate finds painting addictive and sometimes paints a whole collection of works in one session. Rendered in acrylic and spray-paint on canvas or found materials, each painting is unique, although they often suggest ideas for further compositions. Most of Neate's images are loose self-portraits, expressing emotions through fluid lines, colour and brushstrokes with the aim of interpreting the inner soul.

After many years of painting illegal graffiti pieces, Neate switched to these works as an alternative form of public art. He refuses to make a commodity of his art – by not reproducing his designs commercially he makes it impossible to 'sell out' as nothing is for sale. Taking any form of commercialization out of the equation means he feels free to express himself fully.

PATRICK SMITH

Patrick Smith has been creating work specifically for the signposts in the New York neighbourhoods of Uptown, Upper West Side and Upper East Side – areas that aren't accustomed to receiving street art.

Smith thought that the signposts weren't being used to their full potential and so he created designs to fit their tall, thin shape. His wooden structures are made up of interlocking human forms. This theme – the way people relate to one another and their common bonds – occurs frequently in his work.

As an animator Smith had been constrained by the proportions of the movie screen, so he took full advantage of the long and narrow shape of the signposts.

SHES54

SHES54's introduction to graffiti was at the age of eleven, when his enlightened grandmother took him to an exhibition of New York graffiti artists at the Groninger Museum in Groningen. He began with classic graffiti, choosing the name SHES for the flow of the letters, then adding the number 54.

In 1995, he started drawing things in a single line – 'oneliners'. His characters evolved through the years until he became completely immersed in his imaginary world of drawings. Taking it one step further, he created stuffed dolls of his drawings, photographed them and then pasted up the images. In Utrecht, where he lives, there is a lively street scene but not much hand-drawn work. SHES54 likes to keep his work spontaneous, drawing without a safety net – never using a sketch.

He was once locked up for thirteen hours for putting up a single sticker, but he vows to continue trying to make people smile, give out some positive energy and forget daily life.

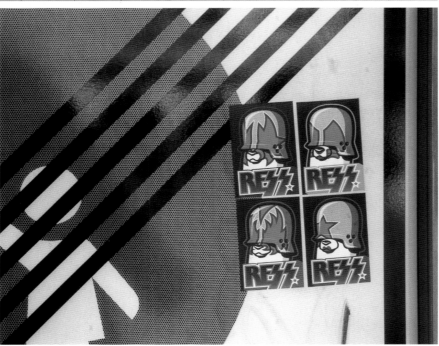

FLYING FORTRESS

Flying Fortress started making graffiti ten years ago but reached a point where he felt there was no progression. Graffiti had become a competition, where spray-can technique was more important than styles and ideas.

Flying Fortress lost interest in graffiti until after art school, when he saw that there were artists out there doing things differently. He was inspired to make something repetitive and a soldier was a good symbol of repetition. The more he duplicated it in posters, stickers and pieces, the more powerful the idea became. As an army, the soldiers also symbolize the occupation of public space.

Not everybody sees the humour behind this legion of bears: 'A logo is a sign that can be taken up by everyone. But not everybody understands it the same way. In Germany my logo is often taken the wrong way. With our historical background of WW2, military symbols are seen as a right-wing message. So my logos sometimes kindle hurried activism by normally passive people destroying my work in the name of I don't know what. But this is a reaction to my work and there is nothing I want more than to make people think about my work. Even if they interpret it the wrong way.'

Top left Painting with Nano4814 and Freaklüb
Top right Stickers with Meat Love

93

THE LONDON POLICE

The London Police (TLP) are three guys, two British (Bob and Chaz) and one American (Garrett), whose smiley faced characters are as much a feature of Amsterdam as plastic tulips and coffee shops. Bob and Chaz originally travelled there with photography portfolios but instead became obsessed with street drawing.

They were attracted to the clean white papered surfaces that an advertising company used to cover up out-of-date posters and found they were perfect spots to display 'The Lads' – the free-flowing, many-headed characters that they had already been doodling on flyers. The Lads are hand-drawn, their perfect curves and clean lines meticulously produced with black marker pens. This striking black and white combination makes them leap out from the surrounding urban space.

Garrett had arrived in Amsterdam from San Francisco and kept noticing these spherical characters on the streets. One night he chanced upon Chaz drawing one. They struck up a conversation, became friends and after three months Garrett was invited into the force.

All three artists draw the characters, which gradually mutate so that no two drawings are the same. After visiting New York, TLP were inspired to go large and more recently they have been producing giant Lads on the sides of buildings.

D*FACE

D*Face's characters have become omnipresent throughout London, and as a result of his travels to other European cities and the neighbourhoods of New York, they have also become familiar faces within the global graffiti community.

D*Face often collaborates with The London Police, sharing their enthusiasm for audacious postering and their taste for a clean black and white graphic style. His campaigns feature two slightly twisted and broken itinerant cartoon characters – the bashed-teeth and droopy-eyed D*Face figure and his winged 'Balloon Dogs'.

He is keen to use as many different media as possible, as well as stickers and posters, and has also screen-printed directly on to the street surface to produce some unique results.

JACE

Jace had been painting for two or three years but found that people couldn't differentiate his paintings from others, so he decided to develop something different. His solution was the multitalented Gouzou: 'At the beginning the Gouzou was really static and I couldn't imagine at this time I could create such a wealthy universe with so many graphic constraints!'

On Reunion Island, where Jace lives, Gouzou has become a local celebrity. People take pictures, steal posters and a lot of children copy the design. Even the tourist guide now talks about him. The problem is that the island is relatively small so the authorities can find him quite easily.

Gouzou interacts with billboards, playing with characters or texts already present on them and also turns up in some spectacular spots that can only be reached by the foolhardy with a climbing rope. For Jace, graffiti is a spontaneous and free form of expression. He's always happy to be surprised by a new artistic action in the street: 'A city with graffiti is a living city. A tree without birds isn't a tree.'

HOERNCHEN

Hoernchen is the German word for both a marmot and a croissant. In the graffiti world, Hoernchen is an acid-green animal resembling a squirrel who patrols the streets of Hamburg. In an age of aggressive marketing, these squirrel hoards take no prisoners in launching a guerilla counter-offensive against commercials, political posters and all the graphic garbage that fills the streets in all the big cities of the world. With the addition of hand-written messages, Hoernchen champions the things it loves and comments on the things it doesn't: 'It's a fight for better images for all eyes, against obtrusive graphics and commercials, for a better graphic thinking for everybody!'

GOMES

Gomes is a Hamburg-based artist who takes full advantage of a screen-printing studio to produce street posters and to run a small label – The Lousy Livincompany – selling his own limited-edition T-shirts. He is best known for his posters, stickers and cut-out drawings of paper drinking cups. These are sometimes accompanied by figures but they also feature a wider cast of characters. His aim is to produce art that draws the eye, capturing the attention of the people in the streets.

The mood of his poetic and unusual street work is more romantic than hard-hitting. He often relates his work to his favourite music, taking inspiration from the lyrics and sometimes quoting song phrases. Gomes also enjoys artistic sparring with friend Alexone. They challenged each other to a painting and postering death match – the result of the first round in Hamburg was a tie, but they are currently preparing for round two.

REGULAR PRODUCT

Regular Product grew up in deepest darkest Melbourne and after some worldwide travel is currently based in Sydney.

At art school he was into making free and accessible artwork – one of his first projects was to make postcards and post them to random addresses from the Yellow Pages. He then moved on to stickers – he failed art college, but he was hooked on street art.

Although street art is automatically associated with the reclamation of public space from corporations in a covert way, Regular Product actually enjoys advertising. He feels that he is playing the same game as the corporations – they just have more resources. As a graphic designer he favours simple colours and bold readable ideas over more complicated stuff. If it doesn't work in black and white, then it won't work in colour.

Part of Regular Product's attraction to this transient art form is that it only comes to life during some kind of interaction with the public – and if that interaction is to rip it down or to draw a moustache on it, then that's cool by him.

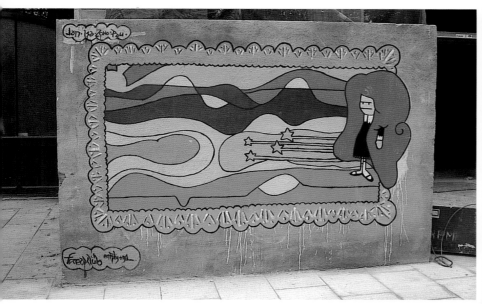

FREAKLÜB

Freaklüb are the combined talents of twin brothers, aka The Shadow Brothers, and the girlfriend of one brother, known as Empty. As graphic designers they are known as Freaklüb Graphics. As street painters they have been developing and painting their trademark character, an orange-haired girl called Aunara, who evolved from a tag by Empty.

When visiting graffiti artists from Toulouse, Miss Van and Vaudou, came to Barcelona to paint with the brothers, Empty became inspired to turn her tagged drawings into paintings. She was shown by them how to use spray with acrylic paint to make sharp outlines, which as an illustrator she was more familiar with.

Soon the wild-haired Aunara grew to be the star of many pieces, executed in bold lines and flat colours inspired by Japanese illustration. These images were accessible. Their simple shapes and elaborate magical backgrounds soon gained many admirers who found this style an antidote to more aggressive styles of graffiti.

MICROBO

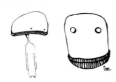

Originally from Sicily, Microbo is now based in Milan, where she has launched an epidemic of stickered and painted microbes on to the surfaces of the city. They originally began as doodles, but over time became more affected and characterized, and she began to use them to communicate her ideas.

Street art has often been likened to a viral disease because it literally spreads across walls, replicates itself and generates more street art through the spread of ideas. Microbes are a good visual symbol for street art as well as the way we communicate.

Microbo herself does not over philosophize. Her microbic creatures are out there to interact with and tease people, created in the spirit of free art. She believes that there should be fewer slogans and commercials and more public art like the frescoes of the ancient world in Mexico, Pompeii and Egypt.

B0130

Based in Milan, B0130 works on the streets with stickers and posters, sometimes stencilling and painting, to create something fresh and positive to liven up the boring grey bits of the city. In the past few years he saw that he could use the tools of his graphics and illustration trade to display his works on the street, blending graffiti with popular culture, art and design and especially with communication.

B0130 works with several trademark characters. The end result is a world populated with multishaped figures, aliens and space crabs. The aliens often have speech bubbles asking questions, trying to get a reaction from the pedestrians. B0130 also likes working collaboratively with his partner in art crime, Microbo, and with the growing fraternity of new Italian graffiti.

ROBOT INC.

Robot Inc. has been creating graffiti and street art for eight years. Brought up in Milan, he started painting trains with his partner Moz in 1996. Then, after some time spent in São Paulo, Brazil, where he painted with artists like Binho and others, he became aware of more diverse approaches to graffiti.

Returning to Milan, he started painting in a new way under the name Robot Inc. His first pieces were gigantic robotic characters, which was a new idea for Milan, a city heavily bombed with tags. Gradually, he has built up a universe of strange characters, working with stickers, posters and stencils. His most emblematic images are figures with Super-8 cameras for heads. As Robot Inc. is a film maker himself, these are a kind of self-portrait.

PLANK

Plank is the alter ego of a Milanese photographer who has found himself increasingly drawn into the world of street actions. The birth of his son had a profound effect on him and he felt inspired to explore ideas, such as chromosomes and the cycle of life. At first he used stencilled images and later painting and postering.

Plank's most memorable work has been with his series based on images of his son. Each year, he has selected a photograph of his son and created a street campaign with this image. The images appear in many forms and sizes, reminiscent of an electoral campaign or perhaps posters of a lost child. The project is now in its third year and Plank's son has become a familiar street icon, acting like a guardian angel for the city.

POCH

Poch started listening to punk in 1986 and was instantly attracted to the graphics that accompanied the movement. It was back then that he discovered the book *Pochoir à la Une*, as well as the work of artists like Blek 'le Rat', Marie Rouffet, Jef Aerosol and Kriki. They inspired him to take up stencilling.

At the end of the 1990s, he reverted to a more minimalist style, closer to the 1980s in its use of stencils, posters, stickers and latex paint. He uses various visual elements alluding to his musical upbringing, such as Two-Tone artwork, punk, skinhead reggae and 1980s rap. His character pieces are often in black and white, matching the period style, and his signature Poch logo would not look out of place on an original ska record label.

OLIVIER

Olivier was first inspired to paint the streets of Paris after seeing an exhibition of the work of Jean-Michel Basquiat. His characters started out as basic forms – two circles, two arms, two legs and two eyes – which he could draw quickly with spray-paint, roller paint and marker pens. After a while they became more complicated – they wore sneakers, had different hairstyles, played the guitar and even made graffiti.

Olivier's aim is simply to share images with people to make them relax, smile and dream. He hopes that people will stop, look at his characters and be happy to see a positive image. It's a passion with the added thrill of risk. He loves feeling like Arsen Lupin (the French gentleman-thief cartoon character) every time he draws on the street with his spray-cans.

WILD THINGS

Opposite Top row: Chair by Debens, bird by Maze, Barcelona; Deer by Civil, Melbourne; 2nd row: Apes by Karski, Netherlands; Dogs by Jerk and Gilbert, Paris; (above) Cat by Cha, Barcelona; (below) Dog by Gilbert, Paris; Bottom row: Dinosaur by Kid Acne, Sheffield; Unicorn by Maya Hayuk, New York; Uh-oh by So Fuzzy Crew, London

This page Top row: Flying cat by Chat, Paris; Rat Landlord by Nome, San Francisco; Bottom row: Flying duck by Civil, Melbourne; Bunny suit by Dmote, Sydney; Elephant by Alexone, Paris; (above) Ape and bird, New York; (below) Penguin on freight train by Alexone, Canada

FREE-FORMS

Graffiti is a community. Artists interact with each other in shared public spaces with unplanned and spontaneous actions. Paintings and posters overlap; images inspire visual or written replies. Graffiti clusters to create collaged compositions of extraordinary inventiveness. New York street artist Swoon describes this artistic hyperactivity as a 'community of actions'.

At a local level, artists get to know each other either personally or by reputation. Viewing the competition can spur people on to outdo each other with wilder ideas. Graffiti feeds on itself. There is a shared sense of belonging. Globally, the graffiti community promotes itself through the Internet, magazines or through exaggerated tales passed on by word of mouth.

Crews and collectives are another communal side of graffiti. Formed from like-minded people, they pool ideas to create big productions, uniting through a common cause. Crews are not new, but with the novel forms and approaches of twenty-first-century graffiti, collaborative pieces can contain some of the freshest and most dynamic ideas. These get-togethers sometimes have a unifying theme, which might be political or visual; at other times the mood is more impromptu. Outlines are sketched and a few jokes and discussions are shared as signs, characters and other elements begin to take shape. People stand back or move round to new areas of the piece to let others add to existing ideas. These informal gatherings of creative people can result in a spectacular uncommissioned mural.

Above Mural by Mutan Clan, Dole

Graffiti is a combination of spontenaity and group dynamics. Erosie from Holland's Sol Crew points out that 'since it is very temporary...two days later it can be gone...an ungrabbable, independent, living in the moment type of art occurs that consists of the participation of a lot of not-linked people sharing the same ideas...pretty cool!'

Collectives like Eindhoven's Sol Crew, France's Mutan Clan, and the ONG Crew in Barcelona take their inspiration not only from classic graffiti but also from a wider spectrum of artistic influences: the Sol Crew bring in elements of Dutch constructivism, the Mutan Clan produce explosions of cartoon chaos and the ONG Crew draw on the fine and applied arts. Precedents for these unconventional graffiti crews did exist in Europe during the 1980s and the early 1990s, such as Barcelona's Los Rinos, who painted strange objects like giant fried eggs and signed their art with target icons. Today free-thinking graffiti groups are found across the globe, breaking free from the 'normal' approach to graffiti. Instead of conforming to the old formula, the walls are free spaces for experimentation with forms, materials, iconographics, characters and naïve typography.

This final chapter looks both at artist collectives who are producing ground-breaking work and at a few free spirits, such as Swoon, who are taking graffiti art in new directions. In the organized anarchy of new collective work and the random poetic scatterings of free art in cities like New York and São Paulo, perhaps we are looking at the future of graffiti and street art.

SOL CREW

Sol Crew are based in Eindhoven, a city with a big reputation in the new graffiti movement. Its members are Sektie, Zime, Bombkid, Late and Erosie, all of whom come from very diverse backgrounds. Their styles are eclectic, but it's the combination of forms that makes the work strong. Although they are all rooted in traditional graffiti, they find inspiration in everything. For instance, Sektie is influenced by old typography, especially vintage hand-painted wall advertisements, and Zime has developed his labyrinthine style from studying Dutch constructivist graphic design.

Erosie feels that the use of symbols in the current wave of street art has relaxed the rules of engagement. Even though logos are as egotistical as tags, there is less fierce competition. Instead people participate by 'adding more "flowers" to the "botanic garden" we call the street'.

EROSIE

Erosie started making graffiti in 1993 but four years later he felt the need to change. He started to think about tags: 'When you have seventeen tags on a wall, why feel the need to add number eighteen when you can add a symbol to the wall that sucks up all the attention?' For this reason Erosie started using a target as his symbol. Other artists, like Influenza and Space 3, influenced Erosie as he began to play with public space, using his targets as literal and visual focus points.

In around 2000, Erosie became interested in the old bike-wrecks that littered Holland's city streets. These bicycles were unwitting public space invaders that he felt compelled to identify through his 'Eroded City Cycles' sticker campaign. The insignia was devised to be a symbolic empowerment for this demobilized army of lost bikes. Erosie continued to use the bike motif and it also began to crop up in his stickers and in quickly sprayed bicycle shadow drawings.

SWOON

Swoon began making art on the streets of Manhattan and Brooklyn in around 1998. She felt that art galleries were suffocating spaces and nothing in them surpassed the beauty of the chaotic street art outside.

Swoon wanted to find a visual language that responded to the environment she encountered. Her life-size paper cut-out figures are usually based on people she knows. They are an attempt to capture the city life that passes them by, a snapshot of a constantly changing scene.

The highly intricate cut paper also reflects the backdrop to her work— the layered and frayed posters that plaster the wall and the decay and random uncontrollable processes of the city. Swoon sees street art as a phenomenon – a force of nature that helps create the textures and the tides of the city. It defines neighbourhoods and marks out territories, reflecting the basic desire to help create the city we live in.

SWOON

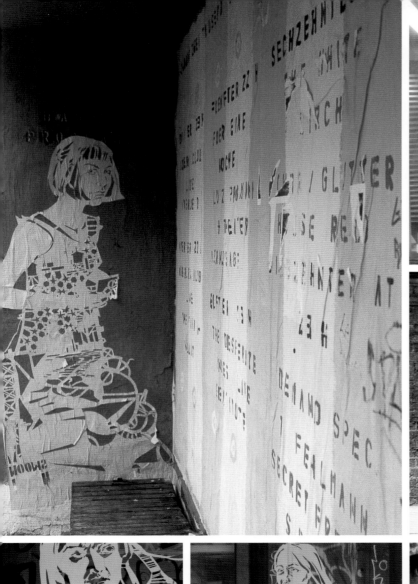

WET SHAME

Headless moose, slabs of meat and mailboxes are just some of the pictorial themes and streams of consciousness you might come across in the work of this Bristol-based collective. Paris, Eko and Mudwig are a loose gathering of artists commonly known as 'Wet Shame'. Paris and Eko are also members of the TCF (Twentieth Century Frescoes), a crew who have produced a huge number of works throughout the UK. Mudwig is the nom de plume of the third member, who is also renowned for his mutant doodling on billboards.

The group acts as an experimental release and a springboard for ideas. Their poster actions are pasted together from separate elements created by the individual artists. There are no rules as to the imagery except they tend to be black and white cut-outs. Some elements are recognizably by a particular artist, such as the typography and patterns of Paris, the birdhouses of Eko and the furred, boned and gristled forms of Mudwig. As the artists continue to work together with group paintings, shapes merge, structures form, and the work takes on a life of its own.

ONG

ONG (Ovejas Negras) is a collective of people dedicated to creation; most of its members are multidisciplined exercisers who find a place of cohesion in graffiti and street art in general. Among them we can find video makers, painters, graphic designers, poets, illustrators, animators, performers and radio announcers.

They specialize in non-conventional urban productions, introducing elements of ephemeral installations, collage and decollage, abstraction and the distortion of existing topics within this type of art.

They tend to interact with people outside the graffiti action sphere, such as inexperienced painters and the homeless. Fate and chance, the relation between the message and the location of the piece, as well as the many challenges of the surface all contribute to the work. Although some of its members disagree with the political stance, the group professes throughout its works a clear libertarian and anti-fascist tendency.

The group's nucleus is formed by the artists Maze, Zosen, Oldie, Debs, Riot, Aviadro, Pez, Mister, Roma, Ali, Sae, Ouf, Flan and Sensible. They regularly collaborate with Xupet Negre, Loon, Chanoir, André, Quién, Rodrigo and, indeed, anyone who wants to paint with them.

p. 118 'Esperanza' by Zosen, Aviadro and Mister, ONG Crew, Barcelona

p. 119 Above: 'Popism' by Mister, Oldie (letters), Riot (cat), Aviadro (machinery and clocks) and Debens (chair), ONG Crew, Barcelona; Below: 'Glamour' by Mister, Germ, Rodrigo and Koalas Negros, ONG Crew, Barcelona

Above 'La Civilizacion Humana esta Condenada' by Zosen and Mister, ONG Crew, Barcelona

Opposite, clockwise from top left 'Petroleo War' by Zosen and Debens, ONG Crew, Barcelona; 'Food not Bombs' by Zosen, Riot, ONG Crew, Barcelona; Chairs by Debens (Keith Haring portrait in background), Barcelona; 'Strange Characters' by Skum, Barcelona

DON'T COPY ME

'Don't Copy Me' was the brainchild of Eko, a graffiti artist based in Pau, France, who is also the mastermind behind Ekosystem, the original new graffiti website.

The idea was to create an independent and international graffiti project that would take place simultaneously across the world. The theme was 'Don't Copy Me', inspired by Dolly, the famously cloned sheep, and was a humorous protest against both the copying within street art and the copying of the graffiti movement for commercial gain.

The event took place at the end of 2002 during just a few weeks timeframe, with artists interpreting the theme in their own way. Graffiti art does copy ideas from itself, but as this collective event proved, original ideas come from individual talents.

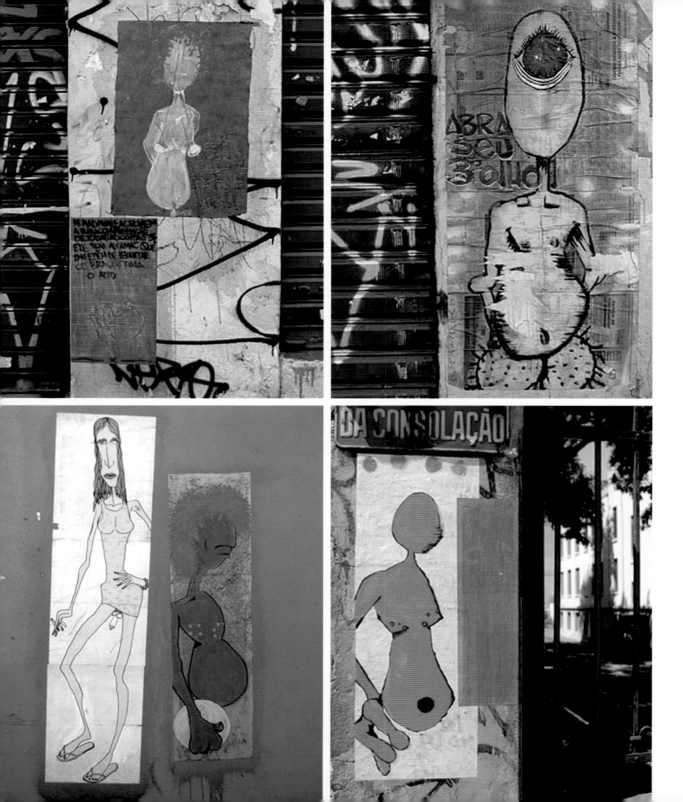

Opposite Figures, São Paulo

This page Above: Figure and abstracts by
Cisma, São Paulo; Below: Chairs, Barcelona

pp. 126–27 Mural by Sol Crew, Eindhoven

p. 128 Mural detail by Barnstormers,
Binghampton, New York

LOOKING FURTHER

Blek, Stak, André, Space Invader, Sam Bern, HNT & Zevs, *Souvenirs de Paris*, Imprimerie Stipa, 2001

Buggiani, Paolo, & Gianluca Marziani, *Keith Haring: Subway Drawings e la New York Street Art*, Mazzotta, 1997

Cano, Genís, & Anxel Rabuñal, *Barcelona Murs*, Ajuntament de Barcelona, 1991

Chalfant, Henry, & James Prigoff, *Spraycan Art*, Thames & Hudson, 1987

Cooper, Martha, & Henry Chalfant, *Subway Art*, Thames & Hudson, 1984

Jace, *Les spasmes urbains*, Jace, 2001

McGee, Barry, Germano Celant, Miuccia Prada & Patrizio Bertelli, *Barry McGee*, Fondazione Prada, 2003

Reisser, Mirko, Gerrit Peters & Heiko Zahlmann, *Urban Discipline 2002*, Getting-Up, 2002

Thompson, Philip, *The Dictionary of Visual Language*, Bergstrom & Boyle, 1980

WEBSITES

www.streetlogos.com

Don't Copy Me www.ekosystem.org

Graphotism www.graphotism.com

Lodown www.lodown.com

Stickit www.stickit.nl

Urban Art www.urban-art.info

Urban Art Official www.urbanartofficial.co.uk

Wooster Collective www.woostercollective.com

Worldsigns Magazine www.ws-mag.com

PICTURE CREDITS

L = Left, C = Centre, R = Right, T = Top, B = Bottom

Above p. 44 R; Action Hero p. 73 BL; Akroe p. 3 2nd row R, pp. 68–9, pp. 74–5 all, pp. 110–11; Alexone p. 77 all, p. 99 BL, p. 109 B3L & BR; Ignacio Arnovich p. 124 all; L'Atlas p. 10, pp. 66–7 all; Beneqoue p. 42; Sam Bern pp. 62–3 all; Betamaxxx p. 2 TR, p. 19 2nd row 2, p. 28 all; Jaques le Biscuit pp. 16–7; BO130 p. 103 BC & BR; Buff Monster p. 3 2nd row L, pp. 80–1 all; Louise Chin p. 73 TL, p. 109 BR(above); Cisma p. 14 all, p. 125 T; Tom Civil p. 18 2nd row 2 and B2L, p. 72 T3L & BR, p. 108 T, p. 109 BL; Cre p. 70 2nd row R; Crustea & Your p. 122 TL; D*Face p. 3 BL, p. 95 T & BL; Steinar Danielson p. 12 TR, 2nd col 2 & 3, p. 18 TL & 2nd row R, p. 71 TL, p. 72 TR & BL; Karen Dews p. 116 L; James Dodd p. 73 T3L; Eko/Pez p. 19 BR, p. 73 T2L, p. 99 BR, p. 122 BR; El Tono & Nuria pp. 64–5 all; Erosie p. 113 all; Etron p. 39 all; Faile p. 30 TL & R; Flowerguy p. 18 TR, p. 19 TR, pp. 32–3 all; Flying Fortress pp. 92–3 all, p. 122 BL; Freaklüb p. 2 BL, p. 3 TR, p. 101 all; Nicholas Ganz p. 2 BR, p. 70 TL, 2nd row 2, 3rd row 1 & BR; Gomes p. 99 TL; Maya Hayuk p. 2 2nd row 2 & 3 & B2L, p. 53 TR, p. 54 L & BR, p. 71 T2L, p. 73 BC, p. 108 BC, p. 109 TR, p. 128; Estate of Keith Haring, courtesy of Paolo Buggiani p. 8 R; HNT pp. 48–9 all; Hoernchen p. 98 TL; Influenza pp. 26–7 all; Jace pp. 96–7 all; Jerk p. 108 2nd row 2; Jey & Jerk p. 9 R; Joystick p. 18 BR, pp. 20–1 all; Karski p. 108 2nd row 1; Kid Acne p. 108 BL; KRSN p. 2 2nd row 1, p. 76 B; Silvio Magiglio p. 3 TL; Mambo p. 19 B3L, pp. 22–3 all; Microbo p. 102 L, BC & BR; François Morel p. 12 TL; Mudwig p. 13 TL & TR Nano4814 p. 2 T3L, p. 84 BR, p. 85 TL, TC & B, pp. 86–7 all; Adam Neate pp. 88–9 all; Vinnie Nylon p. 6, p. 50 BL, p. 52 BR, p. 53 L & 2nd col 2, p. 56 R, p. 114, p. 115 2nd col 2; 108 p. 57 all; OPT p. 9 L, p. 13 B, p. 19 TL; Kerrianne Orriss p. 19 2nd row 1, p. 30 B, p. 31 B, p. 70 2nd row 1, p. 72 TL & 2nd row 3; Pixel Phil p. 18 2nd row 1 & B3L, pp. 33–4 all; Plank p. 104 T, p. 105 TL & B; Plug p. 38 all; Poch p. 106 L, TR & BC; Psalm p. 19 B2L; Regular Product p. 72 BC, p. 100 all; Robot Inc. p. 104 BL; Santy p. 55 B; Señor B p. 3 B2L; SHES54 p. 91 all; Sickboy p. 58 TL & TR & BR, p. 59 T & BL; Patrick Smith p. 90 all; Smok p. 123 B; Sol Crew p. 3 B3L, p. 112 all, pp. 126–7; Sonik p. 12 BL, p. 72 2nd row 1; Space Invader p. 52 T & BL, p. 53 BR; Space 3 p. 1, pp. 24–5 all; Olivier Stak p. 45 all; Stirb p. 123 T; Sums p. 51 all, p. 116 BR; Supakitch p. 122 TR; Swoon p. 115 TL, TR, BL & B2L; Tiñas p. 84 TL & TR, BL, p. 85 TR; TLP p. 94 all; Toasters p. 3 T3L, p. 46 all, p. 106 BR; Hiroshi Tomita pp. 60–1 all; Wood p. 2 TL; Xupet p. 50 T & BR; Jeremie Zimmermann p. 44 1st col, p. 107; Zys p. 15 BL & BR.

All other photography: Tristan Manco.

ACKNOWLEDGMENTS

FOR KERRIANNE

Thanks to all the unknown artists. Thanks to all the artists and photographers who contributed worldwide. Thanks to those who contributed but due to space couldn't be included. Special thanks to those people who inspired and helped along the way.

Artists, photographers and contributors: 108, Abbominvale, Above, Action Hero, Akroe, Alba, Alexone, Ambrio, André, Ignacio Arnovich, Aviadro, Robin Banks, Peter Baranowski, Bäst, Belio Magazine, Beneqoue, Sam Bern, Betamaxxx, Binho, Bild, Blob, BO130, Buff Monster, Paolo Buggiani, Heath Bunting, Jon Burgerman, Cha, Chat, Louise Chin, Cisma, Tom Civil, Lise Colchide, Copy Crew, Cre, Crustea, Steinar Danielson, Debens, Michael De Feo, Jerome (G) Demuth, D*Face, Dlux, Dmote, Eko (Bristol), Eko (Ekosystem), El Cártel, El Euro, El Tono, Emka, Jim @ The Empty Show, Erosie, Etron, Dave Evans, Ewos, Fafi, Faile, Shepard Fairey, S. Faustina, Feek, Flan, Flying Fortress, Freaklüb, Felipe Gálvez, Nicholas Ganz, Gegganoja, Os Gemeos, Germ, Ghaist, Girig, Gomes, Grimm, Maya Hayuk, Keith Haring Foundation, Hear One, Hixsept, HNT, Hoernchen, Human Lost, Christian Huntermark, Influenza, Jace, Jerk, Jey, Joystick, Kami, Karski, Kenji, Kid Acne, Koalas Negros, Krisprolls, KRSN, Lady Bug, La Mano, Last Plak, L'Atlas, Leo, J. Loca, London Police, Los Rodillos, Mambo, Jean Manco, Maze, Meat Love, Microbo, Milk, Patrick Mimran, Miss Van, Mister, Mr Kern, Mr YU3, MKL, François Morel, Jeroen van Mourik (stickit.nl), Mudwig, Mutan Clan, Nano4814, Adam Neate, NMD, Nuria, Vinnie Nylon, Olivier/MDS, OPT, Kerrianne Orriss, Ozmo, Pan Chez, Yann Paolozzi, Paris, Pavia, Pelucas, Pez, Pixel Phil, Plank, Plug, Poch, Nick Pride, Jim Prigoff, Prism, Psalm, Regular Product, Rep1, Riot, Robot Inc., Rodrigo, Sami, Santy, Saru, Marc Schiller (Wooster Collective), Sektie, Señor B, SHES54, Shyam, Sickboy, Sixe, Sküm, Skwerm, Smok, So Fuzzy Crew, Sol Crew, Son103, Sonik, Space Invader, Space 3, Dan Sparkes, Jan Spivey, Stain & Scout, Tony Stiles, Sums, Supakitch, Superyah, Olivier Stak, Stirb, Swoon, Tafek, Tanc, Tiñas, Toasters, Hiroshi Tomita, Twist, Une Nuit, Veenom, Viff, Dan Witz, Wood, Xupet, Your, Zevs, Emile Zile, Zime, Jeremie Zimmermann, Zosen, Zys.